Tom Harrison

THE EYES HAVE IT

a collection of poems

Printed in the United States of America

First Printing, 2024

Library of Congress Control Number: 2024915143

ISBN 979-8-89390-013-2

This book is dedicated

To my family who have stood beside me
and believed in me.

To My wife of 50 years, Shelly,

my daughters Emma and Libby,

and my grandchildren Harrison, Ivy, and Gwen.

Also, to my thousands of tennis students
that through the decades have had an immense impact
on me, more than they'll ever know.

Contents

Middletown, Ohio | 1

Family | 9

Rock and Roll | 25

World | 35

Tom | 47

Middletown, Ohio:

My hometown has given me immense
inspiration all my life and a solid foundation
I continue to build on to this day.

Middletown

There is a town on the banks of the Great Miami, named Middletown. Please take some time and I'll show you around.

This is a town and if it were a boxer it would be the toughest around, yet through much adversity it's managed to keep its feet planted firmly on the ground.

This is a steel town and the sign says Cleveland Cliffs, which is hard to see because it will always be Armco to me.

I grew up in the golden age when steel was king, the town stood tall and her problems were relatively small.

There was always a great buzz around our teams and city pride the Middies brought the town alive.

Basketball, football, it didn't matter the sport the city was always in total support.

Then corporate left town and the boxer fell to one knee, but the bell rang just in time and our town fought back and started to climb.

It was a difficult climb with many obstacles in the way, and many outsiders said impossible it's beyond decay.

And we all know it's about the climb and sometimes we're going to fall, but the climb was the most remarkable feat of all.

The good people of Middletown who are the greatest
that I know, we're not under any circumstances going to
give up or let go.

So after a long climb and many decades of hard work,
the boxer stood tall and started throwing punches once
and for all.

New schools, renewed pride, investment downtown, it's
not totally well, but has turned around.

So now Middletown's future is much brighter than
before and we know there will still be obstacles at her
door.

But the great people of Middletown and that boxer that
we know will fight until the final round and all people
will know how much we truly love this town.

Middletown Tennis Club

It was the Spring of 1958 when this young boy took a trip downtown to a beautiful place, Middletown Tennis Club, it's here I'll state my case.

There were 9 clay courts filled with kids. The boys were fit and lean, the girls were the most beautiful I'd ever seen.

The atmosphere, the joy, the sound of the ball, this was the greatest place in all the land, I couldn't wait to get a racket in my hand.

When I held that racket and hit the ball all my troubles seemed so small. It was a joy and so much fun. I loved to hit and loved to run.

I went every day. My dad took me on his way to work and sometimes I took the bus, ten cents one way, just get me there, I can't wait to play.

Mr. Rice was my coach and he encouraged me in every way. I think he would be so proud if he could see me today.

For you see that seed that was planted all those years ago has grown into a forest that continues to grow.

That wonderful club gave me so much, a sport, a life, a drive and the opportunity to impact thousands of lives.

Sometimes when I'm in town I'll drive down to the old club. It is just a shell of its former self, tattered and decayed, a far cry from its glory days.

I'll sit, close my eyes and I can hear the laughter, the sound of the ball and I think of that young boy who had a dream. Middletown Tennis Club means everything to me.

Middletown High School

It stood proudly for nearly a century, encompassing an entire city block. Middletown High is magnificent in its glory, please come with me now as I tell you its story.

It was stately with pillars standing four stories high, filled with eager students everywhere, a Greek Temple could hardly compare.

It had a beautiful auditorium on one end and a spectacular gym on the other, where basketball ruled. Teams came and tried their best, but most went home losers like all the rest.

We were proud, we were a state power, basketball put us on the map. Steel paid the bills, but basketball brought so many thrills.

The teachers, I will never forget, many made an impression on me, we came and went, I only wish I could tell them now, how much they meant.

The friendships last to this day, we share a close bond, for we are "The Middies" you see, the relationships mean everything to me.

The school taught us much, we learned a lot in class, but the life lessons are the ones that truly last.

We forged into the world on that graduation day and made a lasting impact on society in so many ways.

Then that terrible day came when they leveled our beautiful school to the ground. They can level the structure, they can haul it away, but the memories will endure, they can't tear them down that's for Sure.

So our school is gone and a vacant lot sits quiet, occasionally someone will ask where I went to school. I stand tall and with pride in my voice say; "Middletown High School, Class of '68". We were the best school around and I am so fortunate to have grown up in this town.

I'm proud of the school and the impact that it had. So as each new day beckons and I continue to forge ahead, I'll appreciate and never think twice, I know I'll be a proud Middie for the rest of my life.

Family:

I am so proud of my family and draw inspiration from them daily. My grandparents have been gone for several decades but I continue to think about them every day. My parents gave me everything and a lot of good stories.

Ralph Price

Mt. Rushmore is a magnificent monument in South Dakota depicting great presidents from our past. The monument is built for history and built to last.

I have had many great men in my life that would adorn my Mt. Rushmore. My Dad, my coaches were great mentors, but my Grandfather Ralph Price would be front and center.

Ralph was born January 11, 1890 in Lima, Ohio. He was a buckeye to start, but that state up north captured his heart.

His family vacationed summers in Charlevoix, Michigan and they don't call it "Charlevoix the Beautiful" for no reason, it's beautiful in every season.

After the military (WW1) Ralph met my grandmother, Ida, while working on the railroad in Illinois and with marriage brought joy and settlement in Charlevoix.

Ralph became a farmer in Michigan and operated a canning businesss, he was the boss canning peaches, beets and applesauce.

It's hard to put into words how great of a man he was, he lived life in a wonderful blur, his actions speaking much louder than words.

He was so kind and caring, a grandson's great bliss, he taught us how to drive a boat and even clean fish.

He had a great love of life making friends at every turn. His life was on track, we all loved him and he loved us back.

After my grandmother died he moved to Middletown to be close to us, for most, this would cause great strife, but he took the move in stride, this was the character of the positive Ralph Price.

When I was leaving to go to Vietnam, I didn't know at the time this would be the last I would see him, it was a somber moment and he handed me a 20 dollar bill and said "I wish I could do more" and with tears in my eyes I said, "thank you" and walked away. If only I could relive that day.

I would tell him how he changed my life and how he meant everything to me, how if I could be half the man he was I would be so great, but I'm afraid that day will have to wait.

When Ralph retired for the evening he would walk to bed with a bible in his hand. His actions speaking loud and grand.

I was stationed at Fort Lewis, Washington when I got the call that Ralph had passed. I walked outside, it was cold with a mist, I remember looking up at a street light through my tears and thinking back about all the years. Thinking about all he had meant to me and how I've carried him with me through life. My Grandfather the incredible Ralph Price.

My brother Dave and Ralph had a very close relationship. Dave spent more time than I did in Michigan and has many wonderful memories of time spent with Ralph. He would echo what I've said in this poem. Ralph's nickname for Dave was "Duke".

Christmas 2020

(Or - How A Couch Can Change Your Life)

As we creeped toward Christmas 2020, we juggled many themes, shopping, planning and covid-19.

I'm sure Dr. Fauci would throw us under the bus, if he knew we let Libby, Ben, and Gwen visit us.

We took the chance of infection from out west, wore our masks, prayed and hoped for the best.

All went well until Ben started a puzzle, there was a missing piece now that is trouble.

No need to worry we have Shelly a gumshoe ace, who found the piece in the couch downstairs and closed the case.

Libby left her wedding ring on the table bedside, Gwen thought it would be a fun thing to hide.

We searched the house and things got tense, but we found it in the couch along with 35 cents.

The trip went well and so far we're not a stat, but we'll continue to wash hands and wear our masks.

We will never forget this Christmas of 2020 and the great times we had, we sure miss them all so very bad.

So my advice if you lose your keys, phone, or purse save some time and check the couch first.

Fleeting Glimpse

Time spent with others can be short or long each is precious, each a bond.

When all you have are two days you grab small glimpses any way.

I try to remember that brief exchange, be it a hug, a smile, or basketball game.

This weekend Libby and Gwen came home to honor a fallen friend, it's so sad to know we'll never see him again.

Although our time was short and went fast, I've kept a few memories that I know will last.

Gwen's first trip upstairs to see her room again, her new toothbrush, her M & M's.

Her small voice saying, "I miss you Dad", that was one of the most precious moments that I had.

Libby's visits at night in my room, they meant so much and were over so soon.

Shelly's dedication to her family, she works in a blur, the house is so special because of her.

The snowman out front is a bit small, but to small hands and feet I'm sure it seems tall.

Seeing Ivy and Gwen in the front yard eating snow, that's a memory I'm never letting go.

So as we go through life I hope we all take note of each little moment however remote.

Each day, each moment might not seem like much, but each is special and should be treated as such.

So although our two days flew like a bird in flight, I'll hold on to those glimpses with all my might.

DAD

There have been many great men in my life;

grandfathers, friends or coaches that I've had, however, none can compare to my dear old Dad.

Bill Harrison, was born April 14, 1923 in Middletown, a town where he grew up and thrived. The town stimulated him and brought him alive.

He was raised an only child in a loving family that had history in our town. His cousins, twins Dick and Bob were his best friends around.

After high school Pearl Harbor occurred, our country was at war, school would wait, the Navy came knocking at his door.

His duty was in the Pacific Theater predicting weather for our ships, the three years went by at a very slow clip.

Finally home and off to school at Denison, which was nice, this is where he met my mom, the incredible Nancy Price.

A courtship ensued and in 1948 they were wed, little did they know the grand life that lay ahead.

I was born in 1950 and brother Dave in '53, we were happy to contribute to our parents family tree.

As we grew up Dad was always there with kindness and support. He helped me learn to swim, look up Great Dad in the dictionary and there's a giant picture of him.

He loved music and to sing, spending many years in

a barbershop chorus that made him soar. He always whistled as he came in the front door.

He had a love for sports that brought him alive, be it the Middies, the Reds or the Ohio State Buckeyes.

He had so many great qualities it would take a page to list. He was optimistic, he was gentle, everything a great Dad should be. I'm so fortunate he was always there for me.

So thank you Dad for everything you did and you would be happy to know that Mom is 97 and going strong, however, it hasn't been the same for her since you've been gone.

And you would be proud of Dave and I, we have many of your traits. Your legacy lives on and continues to permeate.

Before I go you should know the Reds lost 100 games and have a long climb, but I know what you would say; "they're going to be just fine".

Christmas

Tis the season, Christmas trees are up, lights are shining bright, school is out, it's a wonderful sight.

For me it feels about the same, but actually something is missing. I'm a little off my game.

I then realized that for the first time in my life of all the wonderful Christmases that I've had, this is the first without Mom and Dad.

Mom passed away this past summer and with that I'm left with only memories of the past, years that went by much too fast.

Christmas was always so special growing up. Mom worked so hard, shopping, cooking and writing the most wonderful cards.

Our house was decorated so beautifully and we always had a live tree decorated with yearly ornaments that were special to me.

Our Grandmother would always come, she didn't travel far, but it always took a couple of trips to unpack her car.

Children were born and each grandchild was given a special gift; Emma an angel, Libby a Santa, Katie a nutcracker, David a bank. Such a nice touch, the kids were excited and appreciated it so much.

It would take a book to document all the great Christmases that I've had, but none were as special as those with Mom and Dad.

So now it's Christmas and I have my wonderful family
to help ease the pain, but I know for me it will never be
the same.

3037 Fairmont Ave.

They say Home is where the heart is and this is truly the case, 48 years in one special place.

Shelly and I were very young when we saw this quaint home, it felt good, it was right, we bought it at first sight.

It felt good from the start, little did we know the stories it would tell. First 7 years it was hot as hell.

No AC at first and no washer and dryer, trips to the laundromats and lots of cold showers.

In 1982 Emma came home, we were truly a family now, house was small, we expanded and knocked out the back wall.

Expansion and hard work ensued, Libby was born in 1986 and that made two.

Thank goodness for photos and videos. When I look back on those years it always brings me to tears.

Countless birthdays, Christmases were on display, but each day was special in its own way.

The girls grew up so fast, those years were so special, but didn't last.

Out the door and off on their own, we could be proud we gave them a great home.

It was quiet now, no more footsteps upstairs, no more "Dad there's a spider over there!"

No more hugs from little girls, no illness through the night. Oh what I wouldn't give for one more sister fight.

But there came new life at 3037, Grandchildren sent from heaven.

Old people like us need our medicine, good diet and rest, but having children around is simply the best.

There are footsteps again upstairs. What a great sound to hear, hugs and kisses bring us such cheer.

So 3037 Fairmont has seen it all, we've accomplished our goals and it sure feels good to be back on spider patrol.

Rock and Roll:

Music Hit me hard in the '60s and has stuck to me like glue. My car is a rock concert on a daily basis.

1964

It was 1964 and I was in the 8th grade, Roosevelt Jr.
High to be exact, playing sports, making friends and
trying not to slack.

Music was a big part of our lives and the new sound
from the radio made us come alive.

This was different, this was unique and from England
they came, long hair, guitars and very funny names.

There were the Beatles that got the start and their
records moved quickly up the charts.

Then came the Rolling Stones their music was bold and
in your face, I ran to buy a record, I could hardly wait.

And buy records I did by the load, which I still have
today I would never ever throw them away.

We grew up, worked, got married and bought a home,
but there was one constant, The Rolling Stones.

Now The Stones had their ups and downs don't get me
wrong, but as the years past they kept producing great
songs.

By now middle age had set in, children were born and
grew, but I still played my records right on through.

I even made a music room dedicated to rock and roll.
Close the door turn it up that was the goal.

The kids moved out and I had done my job, teaching
them many good things; work hard, be nice, don't get to
many loans and never forget The Rolling Stones.

Now old age snuck up on us way too fast. Social Security, Medicare we just hope to last.

But into old age I've stayed a rocker, it's in my blood and it sure beats using a walker.

So now it's 2021 and you'd think The Stones would be dead, but no 60 years later they're on a tour instead.

So I had to go and give it one more shot, miss work, expensive tickets, I don't care one last time I wanted to be there.

So I took the drive to Detroit with Shelly by my side, stood in a long line, my artificial body parts beeped the scanner 3 times.

I had to show a scar to prove I didn't have a gun, not giving up this will be fun.

When they took the stage we forgot our struggles, we forgot our aches and pains, the old songs played we wanted more, for a brief moment it was 1964.

Yes for a brief moment we were young again without a care, there was hope, there were dreams, there was magic in the air.

When the show was over and reality set in we were stiff and sore as we slowly walked out the door.

The spell was broken, it was 2021, thank you Stones for one more good run.

Thank you for working hard and for the great show and thank you for never letting go.

So as I go to work at this advanced age I know I can
win. And if I get tired and my body starts to moan, I'll
fix that and just turn up The Stones.

29

I was raised on rock got that
rhythm in my soul,

I was born to love the beat of that
thing called rock and roll.

The King

Definition of King (Noun)

The male ruler of an independent state, especially one who inherits the position by right
of birth.

There have been kings for centuries, they come as dictators, heads of state, it's been said and others are simply figureheads.

Some fight wars and lead great causes, others are ruthless and take lives and still others behead their own wives.

But in the modern world kings are few and far between, however in 1935 a king was born and little did he know the impact he would have through the radio.

Elvis Aaron Presley was born January 8, 1935 to Gladys and Vernon in Tupelo, Mississippi where Elvis grew up, his mother stayed home and his father drove a truck.

In school he was average. In music, they said he couldn't sing, for sure he wasn't yet The King.

At 13 they moved to Memphis, there was music in the streets. Blues & Gospel, Elvis loved it all, he got a guitar, he was handsome and tall.

Sun Records was in town and he recorded a song as a gift, the rock had hit the water, the waves started to shift.

And the waves became bigger and the records started to sell, the parents thought the kids had definitely gone to hell.

He exploded like a supernova, the music was new and fresh, the kids danced, the girls loved him to death.

He didn't ask to be king and with it can come great toll, but nonetheless he was labeled The King of Rock and Roll.

Then a sad day occurred, Elvis was drafted, Uncle Sam had called, the producers were depressed and the girls just bawled.

Gone for two years this would surely be the end, the music stopped, but a relationship began.

Priscilla was her name, she was young and beautiful, Elvis brought her home with pride, in 1967 she became his bride.

After the military Elvis was back on the scene ready to rock, but his manager said no it's off to Hollywood you go.

Elvis had what it took to sell tickets, star power and good looks, but he was a fish out of water on the screen. They didn't care as long as he brought in the green.

But it was like trying to put a square peg in a round hole, this isn't an actor, he's The King of Rock and Roll.

It took some years, but finally in 1968 a comeback was launched and long overdue Elvis looked great and sounded good too.

Tours were planned and back on the road he went with glee, Shelly and I even saw him in 1973.

He was great and rocked the house, we will never forget that night, music, excitement and flashbulbs that made it so bright.

None of us will ever know how we would handle fortune and fame and even Elvis struggled greatly staying in the game.

Afterall, he was human and maybe that first little pill made him feel better and brought back the thrill.

But one pill leads to another and as the days and years went by, his abilities declined, acquaintances turned a blind eye.

There should have been an intervention to save his life, but this was Elvis, he can deal with all the strife.

So the day came in 1977 when he got his call, went to heaven once and for all.

It was much too soon, the world said goodbye, there was heartbreak, millions cried.

So as I drive in my car I listen everyday to the Elvis channel and remember how he played.

I think of the old days when he was King and the impact he had. I think of what could have been, it makes us all so sad.

So Elvis died much too soon and we wonder what could have been, even with stardom you don't always win.

Thank you, Elvis, we will never forget and you should know your records still sell.

Please save us a room at Heartbreak Hotel.

World:

There is a big world outside of Ohio!
And although there is a lot to be
negative about, I try to always focus
on the positive and the good in people.

Sunrise Sunset

The sun rose the other day in Uvalde, Texas, a rain cloud passed by, a Father wept, a Mother cried.

People drove to work, a dog barked, a child cried in pain, we know nothing in Uvalde will ever be the same.

We all mourn the loss of life, the passing of family or friends, but when it's a child the sadness never ends.

And when it's 19 children in one school, we cry, Dear God oh why, we sit in silence, stare at the wall and simply want to die.

Between the tears we must pause and remember those sweet souls that died in vain. Here are their stories, Here are their names:

Layla Salazar - 11 - "Positive and Energetic," her Mom said, "free spirit and sweet." She certainly would be wonderful to meet.

Tess Mata - 10- When asked about her child, her Mother cried out loud, "I will never hold her again, I was so proud."

Arnerie Garza -10 - Her Mom put it best as she cried, "my little love is flying high."

Xavier Lopez - 10- Life of the party, loved baseball and dance, if only he could have just one more chance.

Nevaeh Bravo - 10 - Nevaeh's name is heaven spelled backward. She loved softball, she was a precious soul, very smart and had just made the honor roll.

Eliahna Garcia -9 - Loved to dance, play sports and host, enjoyed being with her family the most.

Alexandria Rubio - 10 - Straight A student, stayed busy and was never bored, won the good citizen award.

Maite Rodriguez - 10 - Charismatic, goal driven, loved sports and to play, studied and worked hard every single day.

Maranda Mathis - 11 - Enjoyed being outdoors, purple was her color of choice, loved to sing, had a pretty voice.

Jose Flores - 10 - Good with babies and loved to climb trees, his sister said, "He always supported me."

Alithia Ramirez - 10 - For a Bully class she won first place for a drawing titled "Kindness takes Courage" the blue ribbon lit up her face.

Uziyah Garcia - 10 - His Grandfather said it best, and put him on a throne, "He was the sweetest little boy that I have ever known."

Makenna Elrod - 10 - She was a light to all who knew her, she loved to sing and dance and when she hit a softball the other team had no chance.

Jailah Silguero - 10 - Jayce Luevanos -10 - These two cousins described as loving baby angels went through the door their Grandfather opened, he died two weeks before.

Rojelio Torres - 10 - He was a happy child and very smart, his Mother cried, "I have lost a piece of my heart."

Annabel' Rodriguez - 10 - Jacklyn Cazares - 9 - These two cousins would go out of their way to help anyone and had such big hearts, loved sports and especially art.

Eliahna Torres - 10 - Very nurturing and always put others first, each day without her is simply the worst.

Teachers:

Eva Mireles & Irma Garcia

Ask any teacher why they teach and they will rarely say it's about the subject matter or the rate of pay.

No, they will say it's about the kids and making a difference in their lives. When that tragedy hit on that terrible day these teachers were heroes in every single way.

They laid down their lives for the kids and we can only hope as the children died that they found solace in their teachers' eyes.

The sun set the other day in Uvalde, Texas and they say darkness is the worst, you're left with your thoughts and the terrible hurt.

And there's probably nothing worse than walking past your child's empty room in the middle of the night, we need to pray for these families with all our might.

So to the students and teachers at Robb Elementary, who suffered the worst, may you thrive in heaven as you did on earth.

Ukraine

I've witnessed many tragedies in my life; war, hunger, aggression and great strife.

When a country attacks another and it's unprovoked the world is outraged and the world takes note.

Generally I look away and ignore the scene, go on with my life, my hopes, my dreams.

But the images that I see of their misery and pain makes me want to support the people of Ukraine.

This conflict has hit me hard, all the death and dying has left me scarred.

You may ask what one man can do with what he sees, I say "let there be peace on earth and let it start with me".

I know in the enormity of all this I'm just a grain of sand, but I'm going to do what I can to help with the mess. It hurts to see people in such distress.

These are good people with families and a country they love, fighting a country so big. We have to help and give them a chance to live.

I know it seems so far from where we are and may not seem like our concern, but we share the same planet and just can't watch it burn.

I know the day will come when I pass on and I hope to see all my family and those that were close to me.

But when I'm done with Family greetings, I'll ask God to let me see the people of Ukraine. I'll be honored to tell them I shared in their pain.

I will tell them they showed the world how great a people they are and how they made a guy from Ohio see there can be peace on earth and it will start with me.

So as you read this I hope it rings a bell that peace on earth can start with you as well!

Looking Down In Life

There seems to be a problem.

There seems to be despair.

People looking at their phones totally unaware.

Now there could be a fire, a full moon, or a look from the opposite sex.

But they'll never know cause they've gotta check that text.

Before phones a man would walk tall, head held high, enjoying life, observing the sky.

Now the view is a downward bend, I wish they would look up now and then.

People even look down as they drive. ...please look up and keep us alive.

Neck doctors are enjoying the trend as they rake in the bucks...buying big houses and fancy trucks.

I guess there are some advantages to the downward gaze...they can check their shoes, avoid land mines, and check for cracks to avoid breaking their mother's back.

There is so much to see away from your phone...the world is big and great enjoy the view before it's too late.

Put that phone down you'll enjoy the prize and we can even see your beautiful eyes.

So my advice, Look Up, and don't press your luck. ..you'll be very thankful you avoided that truck!

The Eyes Have It

I go through life and my tears will start, not from sadness or a broken heart

No it's not that I'm hurt or upset. It might be a human struggle or someone I've met.

When the music plays and I shed a tear it takes me back to yesteryear.

I may sing out loud or think of those who have passed on. - it all comes back those wonderful songs.

Our mask wearing has a benefit for me and it's not controlling a disease or allergy sneeze.

No - It's now that the eyes stand out, and they tell a story to behold, looking at them. never grows old.

Now I'm not a rich man and I don't travel afar and I don't live in a big house or drive a- fancy car.

But I get to look into the eyes of children everyday and the whole world is right there, hopes and dreams, nothing can compare.

So the eyes have it for me, whether they're teary or dry they tell a story - might make you cry.

So as I wrote this and you read, please excuse my poor grammer and misspells for you see I wasn't seeing quite well.

Tom:

Personal writing tells my story and experiences. I know each day is a new chapter and I will continue to write, hopefully for years to come!

JUNIOR HIGH SEASON 2019

We have a team of girls that can do it all; Study,
Socialize and Hit a Tennis Ball.

We started the season against Miamisburg on August
19, we mowed them down and quickly left the scene.

Sycamore was next, their colors are green and white, we
conquered them without much fight.

Plains Jr. High was next, we played in some field, their
team tried hard, but had to yield. Miami Valley was on
the run, we beat them badly, it was really fun.

We rolled into Mason, the weather was dry, we beat
them easily and made them cry. Emma was sick, we
played in her name, Mason Jr. High Tennis, will never
be the same.

Centerville thought they could put up a fight, they were
wrong, we blew them out of sight. They call themselves
the Elks and I'm here to say Panthers eat Elk for
Breakfast everyday.

We went to Liberty Jr. High, we scheduled a Bout, we
hit them so hard their braces fell out.

Back to Miamisburg, they shook in their shoes, they
tried hard, but still had to lose.

Down to Hopewell, which had little Hope, we took care
of business and that's no joke.

Miami Valley finished up the year these girls deserve a
really big cheer.

None of the teams had much of a chance, we were on a roll and ready to dance. To the 7th graders, next year you lead the pack, hope the other teams invite us back.

To the 8th graders, we will miss you, I fear, and I know we will all shed a tear. Just know we will never forget this team, this season has truly been a dream.

The Bug

There seems to be a Bug in our midst, causing us havoc, giving us fits.

It's done about everything that we know, closing schools and stopping shows.

It's made us wear masks wherever we go, can't kiss or hug, quite a blow.

But we can't let a dumb Bug get us down, stand up, fight and remove that frown.

We need to stay positive and stand tall, it's just a dumb Bug we can smash after all.

Treat it like a tennis point, run it all over the place, And when it comes to the net, smash it in the face.

Now the Bug seems quite worried as a vaccine draws near, we will win this fight, that is clear.

So when the day comes and we are Bug free, Stand Close Together, the drinks are on me.

SunShine

They come with sadness and seem to be in distress, illness?, perhaps they flunked that last test.

Perhaps they scraped their knee, falling off the slide, or missed the bus and had to bum a ride.

No, it's not any of those things. They're down and out because of the rain.

Now it might rain, sleet or snow, and the clouds may close in, if that's your fear you're going to be miserable most of the year.

I have an idea, to turn it around. Make your own sunshine and remove that frown.

Put a smile on and stay upbeat, even the dreary days can be pretty neat.

If it rains you don't have to go far, and you can even let it wash your new car.

The ducks will rejoice and swim with glee, even the umbrella salesman will collect a good fee.

If it snows, a blanket and good book work best, and you could even get some much needed rest.

Shovel the walk and help out at home, hot chocolate works great at warming your bones.

Let the sun shine in your mind, if it's cloudy and grey the people around you will like you that way.

So my advice, if it's not sunny, warm and clear, make
your own sunshine and enjoy the new year!

54

Retirement

Hardly a week goes by that someone doesn't ask when are you going to retire Tom, have fun, play golf, soak up the sun?

Although I appreciate their concerned look they need to know I'm not playing by the book.

Authors, musicians and artists enjoy earning a wage and their accomplishments are celebrated at their advanced age.

Although my accomplishments aren't made with paper, paint or sound, mentoring a young person through tennis is the greatest feeling around.

As a coach I enjoy stimulation everyday. My players are my team and we work hard together to accomplish all our dreams.

The bond between coach and student is special and when they let their wall down and allow you into their life the stars feel within reach, you really can't find that laying on a beach.

I'm very happy for those that have moved south and drink everyday, but I'm happy on the court and will continue to stay.

I'm sure the day will come, I'll put my racket down, retire and enjoy the so called perks but please not yet I can't wait to go to work.

Greetings

Most of us receive greetings each and everyday, mostly in gracious and very loving ways.

To be greeted with kindness and respect is gratifying and something one doesn't soon forget.

When I received a letter from the President of the United States I knew what it was and would truly seal my fate.

It was a letter that I feared the most and not an assignment to some important post nor an invite to a Rose Garden toast.

The letter read greetings you are hereby ordered to report for active duty in the Armed Forces of the United States of America.

Now what kind of greeting is that? Not very kind to say the least and our country was at war not peace.

This letter struck fear when thousands of our boys were coming home dead each year.

I put on my best optimism hat, decided I would never slack, jumped in my car and went to buy a six pack.

A month later after being sworn in I was on a plane to Fort Leonard Wood, this is where my story begins.

It was dark and as cold as you could get, a perfect location for a horror film set.

Training started and the drill sergeants called us meatheads, we got no slack, however we called them much worse behind their backs.

Two weeks into training I slipped on ice and fell, dislocated my shoulder, hurt like hell.

Moved to a rehab platoon for an 8 week stay, recovery, rehab and back to training someday.

Now I never played volleyball for all it was worth, but during those 8 weeks I played more than any human on earth.

First breakfast then volleyball until lunch, then again until dinner 8 hours in all, I played one armed, could even slam the ball.

48 hours a week on the court, we were lean and mean the olympics beckoned, but we couldn't leave the scene.

My shoulder was better now and back to training I went with a whole new batch of guys going to give it one more good try.

And what a tough experience it was not for the lame or meek, but I know I can do it, it's only 8 weeks.

Marching, tear gas, shooting lots of guns I have to admit throwing hand grenades was actually kinda fun.

Finally my time in Missouri was winding down, I had survived 8 weeks of hell and lots of volleyball as well.

My next assignment read Artillery, Fort Sill Oklahoma a combat role, not good, made me want to stay at Fort Leonard Wood.

It was summer now as I took a bus due west not knowing what to expect hoping for the best.

If you like hot weather Oklahoma is the place for you, hot as the sun, no AC and no fun.

And fun was not to be had shooting artillery everyday in the heat, blowing up the countryside I was totally beat.

In 8 weeks of training we did many things, I learned to drive a tank. I wished I could take one home, that would cause quite a fright! Not very fast, but I could run all the lights!

Now the moment of truth has arrived, my next assignment might determine if I live or die.

It could be Germany or some other peaceful place, but no, Vietnam is what the paper said, my heart sank as I slowly hung my head.

I prayed to God to watch over me, I promised him many things; I'll go to church more, drink less, I'll even help old ladies in distress.

And I know I had many others praying for me that I could never repay, I just hoped I could make them proud each and every day.

So after a brief trip home I was long gone and off to fight the VietCong.

Greetings (Part Two)

(Part one of my story I wrote as a poem, but Part Two (The War Year) I decided to write as a story. It's difficult in poem form to go into detail and sometimes you omit an idea because you can't get it into a good flow or rhyme.)

It was a long plane ride to Vietnam with a stopover in Alaska and Japan. As Dorothy so eloquently said in the Wizard of Oz; "Toto I don't think we're in Kansas anymore." I sure wasn't in Ohio anymore nor anywhere else in the United States for that matter. This was a war torn third world country where bicycles were the primary source of transportation and water buffalo pulled plows in the field.

After being processed and moved to a base we settled in to find out where we would be sent. I knew I would go to a firebase somewhere and give support to the ground troops. While waiting we heard that they were short FDC guys (Fire Direction Control) and should inquire. This would be a much better job than being a gunner so myself and two other guys checked it out.

They were willing to take us and this turned out to be a really good opportunity. I was assigned to a firebase called "Rawhide". This was a long hill basically in the middle of nowhere. We had a battery of medium range guns and a battery of long range. The fighting was going on around us and we gave support when needed. Since I was now FDC I was located in an underground bunker where we had communications and worked up all the data for the fire missions.

This sure beat the physicality of firing the guns. We worked 12-hour shifts, 7 days a week, of course there are no days off in a war zone. Our hill was surrounded by barbed wire and land mines well-guarded so no one was going to walk in without a fight. They would occasionally fire rockets or mortars our way and we would retaliate, over all we were pretty safe. I settled into a routine and was lost for quite a while with all the data, but when you do something 12 hours a day you eventually catch on. I actually became very good at calculations and talking on the radio. The ground troops would call in for support. We would get their location, work up the data and send the information to the guns. This was my job for the next year. Off time I mostly rested, although difficult with loud guns going off all hours.

Letter writing was my main pastime and I wrote a lot and I appreciated so much all the wonderful letters I received during my time in the service. That's what really kept us going. Fortunately we also had beer although warm it was something to look forward to after a shift.

I would like to say at this point that I met many hundreds of great guys from almost every state. There were also the bad guys, drunk, drug addicts and convicts that you kept a low profile around, but the vast majority were great and I know they went home and had very productive lives.

So we counted down the days and dreamed of many things; family, good food, a comfortable bed and girls! We referred to the United States as the WORLD. And we were constantly saying what we were going to do

when we returned to the World. After several months
at "Rawhide" we got word that they were closing down
the base and we would be moving. This was a lot of
work to pack everything up and transport everything via
helicopter to our new base. It took about a month and
although hard it was worth it. We loved the new base.
Safer area, less fire missions and we actually had a bar
with local Vietnamese girls serving drinks! This is where
I finished out my duty. So finally the day came when I
would go home. After some sad goodbyes, to my friends
and the Vietnamese girls, I was ready to head home.

I could go on and on about our terrible handling of the
war and how we just left those people, but that's for
another time.

I am now on a plane going down the runway and as
the wheels leave the ground a loud cheer goes up as if
our favorite team just scored a touchdown. Back in the
good old USA I flew into Cincinnati. Mom and Dad
were there to greet me and with tears in our eyes I could
finally say Home at Last, thank God Almighty I'm
home at last.

And of course Dorothy said it best; "There's No Place
Like Home!'

P.S.

Fifty years later looking back on my experience I have a
different perspective than I did at the time.

The military taught me many good things - discipline,
a good work ethic and an appreciation for what I have.
Since that time I've worked hard and never taken
anything for granted. I also learned that life can be

taken away at an instant and to appreciate each day. I am also proud to have served this great country!

And

I always root for Army to beat Navy in the annual football game!

I dedicate this story to the over 40 thousand soldiers who never came home. My heart goes out to them. I will always grieve for them and their families. They made the ultimate sacrifice and will never be forgotten.

About The Author

Tom Harrison lives in Dayton Ohio and is the owner of the Tom Harrison Tennis Center in Springboro, Ohio.

Tom was born and raised in Middletown, Ohio where he developed a passion for tennis at a very young age.

In his spare time, he enjoys sports, music, and spending time with his family. He also enjoys writing poetry. His grandfather and mom were poets before him, and he's proud to carry on the family tradition.

9 798889 390013 2